D1635972

A BIG EASY CHILDHOOD

Memories of Growing Up
In Enchanted New Orleans

Guy C. Lyman, III

ISBN: 978-0-578-15122-9

This first edition published by Monkey Hill Publishing,
New Orleans, LA.

Design and layout by Lindsey Roussel

IN MEMORY OF MY FATHER,
GUY C. LYMAN, JR.

CONTENTS

1. INTRODUCTION..................................3
2. WHERE ELSE BUT NEW ORLEANS?.......................5
3. WEBSTER STREET.................................10
4. EGGING THE DEKES..............................19
5. THE EASTER DUCK 22
6. MCKENZIE'S....................................25
7. THE CORNER GROCERY............................28
8. SUMMERTIME....................................31
9. STREAKING.....................................40
10. THE RIVER.....................................42
11. MARDI GRAS....................................44
12. THE FRENCH CONNECTION.........................49
13. THE LAKEFRONT................................ 53
14. MAIDS.. 58
15. RAY'S ROLLERAMA.............................. 65
16. THE AVENUE................................... 68
17. FOOD... 73
18. PHILIP STREET................................77
19. SPORTS.......................................83
20. SHOPPING.....................................87
21. AUDUBON PARK.................................92
22. HURRICANES................................... 96
23. DECAY.. 99
24. A PRAYER FOR NEW ORLEANS.....................101

Introduction

This is a book about growing up in New Orleans. You won't find much about the French Quarter, jazz funerals or history, because they simply didn't figure largely in the lives of the city's children. Anyway, there are more than enough books that address these subjects.

I've limited myself to the period between my birth and the beginning of adolescence, from 1960 to around 1973. Of course, I've had wonderful experiences in the city since then, but they don't belong here.

When it comes to our city, we New Orleanians are sticklers for accuracy, so I apologize in advance for any errors or distortions.

In deference to today's extreme sensitivity to class consciousness, I have a couple of things to say to head off any suggestions that my recollections are tainted by privilege. First, my family was not wealthy; we were an upper-middle class family struggling to cover five private school tuitions amidst a broken-down public school system. Moreover, what

3

privileges we did enjoy were due to the heroism of my father,
whose own father was a suicide and mother an alcoholic.
From the age of twelve on he essentially reared himself and his
younger brother, won a scholarship to Tulane University,
graduated Phi Beta Kappa in only three years and earned a
scholarship to the law school, where he achieved Order of the
Coif and Law Review. He then worked doggedly for years to
help build what would be one of the city's finest law firms in its
day. Nobody should begrudge this man any advantages he
ultimately was able to give his children.

I don't address the racial issues New Orleans faces here
either, though I am certainly not blind to them. Like many, I
hope the remaking of the school system will go part-way
towards addressing these problems, but this remains to be
seen. At any rate, the intention of this book is to tell about a
New Orleans childhood from one person's perspective, with
the inevitable limitations and blind spots, and not to change
the world.

Where Else But New Orleans?

Because this is a book about how New Orleans shaped my childhood and not an autobiography, I wouldn't spend time on my ancestors if they weren't such interesting New Orleans stories themselves.

My grandmother on my father's side, Helen Baird, was William Faulkner's great love when he lived in the French Quarter in the 1930's. She was the basis for heroines in his first two novels, *Mosquitoes* and *Soldier's Pay*, and he hand-lettered and illustrated a long poem in book form for her: *Helen, A Courtship.* Characters reminiscent of Helen also appeared in later novels, including *The Wild Palms,* for which he won a Nobel Prize. He never forgot her.

Helen was a genius, an artist and a rebel, a drinker and smoker who cut her hair short and looked like a pixie. When I was very young, before she died of cancer, my siblings and I visited her occasionally with my father; she lived in a nursing home somewhere out in the suburbs. I remember the ribbed

plastic cigarette case my father used to sneak her cigarettes. I
didn't like those visits. She had gnarled, tobacco-stained
fingers, sunken eyes and a rough voice, and she scared me. I
didn't know what an interesting person she had been; my
father never spoke about his unhappy past. He often said, and
not out of pride: "the Lyman family begins with me."

Faulkner wanted desperately to marry Helen but she married
my grandfather, the original Guy C. Lyman, instead. He was
apparently quite charming if a bit conventional, and he, Helen
and Faulkner remained friends, spending time together in
Pascagoula, Mississippi. My grandfather helped him get the
southern black dialect down. Later, Guy and Helen would
move to Denver with their two boys, where her drinking and
erratic nature, in combination with mounting business
pressures and his own private demons, drove him to suicide.
Helen and the boys moved to Tucson and her drinking
continued, but my self-reliant father would return to New
Orleans years later on a Tulane scholarship, where he would
meet my mother.

My grandparents on my mother's side were an entirely
different story. Daniel Manget was a handsome, debonair
gambler in a white linen suit. On a business trip up East, he
had met a beautiful Irish redhead from no special stock but
exuding a profound strength of character and had taken her
back to New Orleans to marry her. This was my grandmother,
Marjory.

Dan was a superior tennis and golf player, and so strong he once removed the pilings from a ruined pier by locking his arms around them and rocking them loose. I recall his accidentally making me cry as I hand-wrestled him while he talked to my parents, crushing my hand with his pinkie finger.

Together the dashing couple became the toast of the town. They founded St. Martin's School, and the Icebreakers and Valencia clubs for teens. They threw lavish parties and entertained a stream of dignitaries visiting New Orleans. Dan reigned as president of the powerful Cotton Exchange, and bought himself a new Cadillac every year.

Then the New Orleans speculator Tom Jordan decided to unload his cotton shares, starting an avalanche, and the cotton market crashed. Being a gentleman, with a sense of responsibility for the market over which he presided, Dan threw his entire personal fortune into an effort to shore it up, buying up as many shares as he could. It didn't work.

Ruined, he refused to declare bankruptcy in order to get a new start. His name was on the notes he had signed, and to him this meant something. He spent the rest of his life working to pay off his debts, doing anything he could, including peddling real estate in the hinterlands of Mississippi.

When Dan died, my father flew to see the remaining creditors. All forgave the debts rather than press them against Dan's widow Marjory, expressing profound admiration for a man they considered the last of a dying breed.

All but one, that is. Much later, my brother remembers finding my father drinking alone at night, and asking him what was wrong. The one creditor who had refused to forgive Dan's debt had died at long last, and nothing at all was wrong; my father was enjoying a few celebratory cocktails.

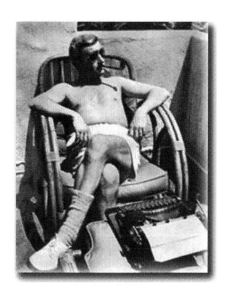

William Faulkner as a young man in New Orleans, where he courted my grandmother in the French Quarter. She wouldn't marry him, but he modeled the heroines of three books on her anyway.

I enjoy the context into which I was born - the gambler in the white linen suit, Faulkner's French Quarter love interest, even the associated calamities. Where else but New Orleans?

Webster Street

I'll skip my first few years, most infancies being fairly
homogenous as long as there is love and food, and get directly
to the next and more interesting phase of my New Orleans
upbringing, which centered around two blocks of Webster
Street near Audubon Park. My parents lived first in a small
house in the 900 block, then moved to a larger house in the
1000 block as the family grew.

Living across the street was Margaret Orr, our favorite
babysitter because she was not much older than we were. She
would later become a popular New Orleans TV
meteorologist. Down Camp Street in a tiny pink box of a
house (still there) lived the wonderful Miss Daisy, with her
boxes of sea-shells and magic garden in back. Around the
corner was an orphanage, a concept so mysterious to my
siblings and me that it might as well have been Mars. We were
a little afraid of it, but once spoke to a resident through the
chain-link fence and found to our surprise that he was pretty
much like us.

Many of my fondest memories of this period involve the Callahans in one way or another. The Callahan family lived in a defiantly neglected house on our block, a dark hive of twelve unruly kids and their hard-bitten parents along with various sinister love interests and hoodlums who came and went day and night in rumbling muscle cars.

The Irish have such a long and rich history in New Orleans that they long ago melted into the fabric of the city, their Brooklyn roots contributing greatly to the city's now ubiquitous "Yat" accent. But the Callahans of my youth were of the uncut, rough-and-tumble sort that I imagine populated the so-called "Irish Channel" between Magazine Street and the river before giving way to black families, and later, partial gentrification by white ones.

The kids were usually dirty and always ill-clothed. Often the boys were shirtless. Their noses ran a lot, I recall. They behaved badly, cussed and devoted a great deal of time to thinking of new ways to get into trouble. In other words they were ideal playmates, and my best friends through the Webster Street years, to my parents' dismay.

My siblings and I were banned from entering the Callahans' home. I suffer a delayed embarrassment now over this, but at the time it seemed perfectly rational. If their house was scary to me, it must have been a nightmare to my proper parents. But to their credit they let the Callahan kids play at our house freely, and the younger ones among the twelve spent much of their time with us.

This was the mid-Sixties, and looking back now I can make sense of some things that were mysterious to me then. I remember illegally entering the Callahan home to the delight of a teenage Callahan girl, Joyce, who toured me around and proudly showed me her 45 rpm records. I read the title of one of them aloud as "Smock Gets In Your Eyes" and she laughed, to my great embarrassment – both because I had proved myself illiterate, and because even at my young age I was aware of her dark beauty and had humiliated myself in her presence.

I recall Joyce's boyfriend wearing a t-shirt emblazoned with "Da Nang" and some military jargon, which I evidently found exotic enough to remember to this day – though at the time, I didn't know it meant he'd seen action in the Vietnam War. In fact, I didn't know there *was* a Vietnam War, much less anyone fighting in it.

Once, the word got around the neighborhood that Mrs. Tubbs, who lived across the street, had opened the door only to be slapped in the face by Mrs. Callahan, who had caught wind of a supposed slight. Another time, and I witnessed this, Mrs. Callahan confronted my mother with an accusation that a Lyman had stolen one of her kids' toys. "Your precious angels would never do anything like that, now would they?" she hissed when my mother indignantly denied it. Mostly, however, we got along – the kids, if not all the grown-ups.

   If you were fortunate enough to be a child during or before this time, you'll remember that kids were allowed to roam freely until dark, when they came home to dinner. I'd rank the loss of this freedom as the second greatest destroyer of the joys of childhood, right behind computer games and television (which in the Sixties had still not devoured our afternoons and summers, but would soon enough). I doubt that there are more child molesters today than there were back then, but it's rare to see kids allowed to gambol about barefoot and free anymore, at least in polite neighborhoods. The kids seem happy to anesthetize themselves with electronic media, and their parents are glad to have them safely home between soccer practices and other planned activities. What a pity. Counting both sides of the street, there were thirty kids on our one block of Webster Street, and you could be sure that at least some of them would be out on the sidewalks at any given time.

   In a game we called "Runaway Girl, Runaway Boy," the Callahans, my siblings and other neighborhood kids ranged barefoot (we rarely wore shoes, in fact) over many city blocks, taking turns capturing members of the opposite sex by hunting for them in alleyways and backyards and chasing them down. We also played a lot of "Kick the Can," bursting from bushes in an attempt to kick over a carefully-watched can while its guard was distracted chasing other attackers to "freeze" them. The best time was dusk, when the coolness set in and excited our blood, just before our mothers called us in.

Back then most yards were less manicured than they are today. Each city block was to an adventuresome child a self-contained kingdom of hideouts, passageways, walls that could be climbed and fences that could be squeezed through. Many backyards were riotous with vegetation, New Orleans being essentially a tropical city, so that you might create a secret clubhouse in a bamboo patch or a hedge that had grown wildly and never be seen. To this day I could easily draw detailed maps of the blocks on which I lived as a child and their secret places and passages. When I drive past large, brick, cookie-cutter homes in sterile, polished suburban neighborhoods, I feel sad for the kids who live there.

In the next block lived the infamous "Debbie and Veronica," the children of another dubious family my parents lumped in with the Callahans. They were indeed bad girls, and we were warned away from them. Nevertheless, I clearly recall our sneaking into their house to watch the forbidden TV show "Dark Shadows," a vampire soap opera we couldn't resist, despite the fact that it terrified us. I watched it from behind a chair, peeking out only occasionally. The theme song alone was enough to instill terror; I remember every note of it.

An end came to our surreptitious visits to the home of Debbie and Veronica when one day my older sister went missing and was searched for in each home and up and down

14

every block to no avail, and with increasing alarm. She had been told by one of them to hide under my mother's bed and not to utter a word as the search went on. My sister caved and revealed herself as my mother wept to the police on the phone, and that was the end of Debbie and Veronica, at least as far as we were concerned.

Though my parents were not big picture-takers, being more inclined to enjoy the moment rather than record it for future reference, we do have a faded photo somewhere of a sort of carnival or circus that a bunch of neighborhood kids put on for neighborhood parents in our backyard. I believe the marquis act was our dog Brumby stepping over a stick held very low. What is striking to me about the photo and so wonderfully New Orleanian is that the parents are decked out in full tuxedos and evening gowns, martinis and cigarettes in hand (remember, this was the late Sixties). It was a cool crowd, still young and good-looking, and evidently good-humored as well.

Charles Buchanan lived on Calhoun Street, maybe eight blocks away, and though an "uptown" kid and son of an august Tulane history professor he shared with the Callahan boys an attraction to deviance. So of course I was drawn to him as well. His home was a block from Audubon Park, and we spent a lot of time there climbing its huge, moss-draped oaks and searching for golf balls. He had two older brothers who were frightening to me, and two pretty hippie sisters. Beneath one of the floorboards in the upstairs hallway was a secret

compartment where his contraband of various sorts was
stored.

Sometimes we invaded the campus of Tulane University in
our bare feet trying to infiltrate forbidden rooms. We'd blow
things up in his basement when his mother wasn't around, and
once blew someone's metal garbage can to smithereens with
some kind of primitive explosive device. Often we'd ride our
bikes to the even then old-fashioned hardware on State and
Magazine, amazingly still extant as of this writing, to buy pea-
shooters. Then we'd buy bags of small white beans from the
grocery store, which were more affordable than the "official"
peas sold with the straws in addition to being of a higher
velocity. We'd walk about shooting at anything that moved,
including cars, children and pets.

One day we came across a very large pockmarked boulder on
the Audubon Park golf course unlike anything we had ever
seen. New Orleans is entirely flat and built on alluvial silt, so
you won't see a boulder unless it has been dragged from
somewhere else. And who would want to drag one this large
anywhere? To us it was other-worldly. In fact, from its strange
appearance and my thin familiarity with geology, I concluded
(as had other children) that it had come from outer space, and
we greedily collected broken bits from around it. It was only
recently that I learned the "meteorite" was an example of iron
ore brought in from Alabama for the World Cotton
Centennial of 1884. So it really *was* pretty exotic.

This large iron ore sample from an old exhibition, still to be seen on the Audubon Park golf course, was believed by most New Orleans kids to be a meteorite.

A couple of weeks after Katrina, I found myself driving slowly through the city's streets drinking bourbon at two in the morning (yes, it was safe: the streets were utterly empty). I was feeling nostalgic and sad for the city, and I decided to see if I could find the "meteorite" - though I had no idea where in Audubon Park it might be.

I drove to what had been the Buchanans' home - the family is long gone - got out of my car, and walked up the street and into the park. I walked beneath torn, ragged oaks until I

17

reached the road running around the park, and crossed it to the lagoon. There was a glowing mist hanging over the park. In the center of the lagoon was an island where a motley crowd of birds, including the white ducks much loved and well fed by local children, build nests and roost. This night they were in a frenzy of some sort and the air was filled with a cacophony of squawking and screeching. I guessed that their nests and territories had been thrown into a shambles by the hurricane, and this chaos was the result.

At any rate, the crazed birds, the stripped trees and luminescent mist combined to give the night a surreal quality. But the true magic was the almost magnetic attraction that pulled me along the edge of the lagoon until I could make out in the darkness a stone bridge that led to the golf course on the other side. I crossed the bridge and began walking across the misty grass as if I were being led. And there before me, looming out of the fog, was the "meteorite." I sat by it for a long time, with whiskey tears in my eyes, thinking of Charles Buchanan, the Callahans, the heartbreaking charm of this city, and how fortunate I was to have grown up in it.

Egging the Dekes

The "Dekes" were the Delta Kappa Epsilons, a fraternity of rowdy drinkers whose chapter house was located in a residential area on Henry Clay Avenue. On Halloween night it became a tradition among area kids, who knows why, to "egg the Dekes" - throw eggs at their white wooden house, which would then have to be laboriously scrubbed by the fraternity's pledges.

Eventually the Dekes fought back. They dug a pit in their yard, filled it with water and added red dye along with various unmentionable ingredients. Then they hid and waited for the kids to show up.

To his shock and horror, the first kid who crept through the darkness to hurl an egg found himself chased down, tackled, and transported by burly college boys to the pit, into which he was unceremoniously tossed. Then another kid, and another, were caught and dyed. By the end of the night, uptown kids had gotten the message. And so had their mothers.

But as these things go, the danger of the dye pit became its own enticement. At our young age, we didn't know what a "Deke," or even a fraternity, was. To us, Dekes were large, dangerous thugs who guarded their house like trolls under a bridge. They terrified us. So egging the Dekes became a rite of passage, a test of manhood. The goal was to pelt the house with at least one egg and scamper away quickly enough not be caught.

It's anybody's guess how the tradition of "egging" the Deke (DKE) fraternity house on Henry Clay Avenue got started, but it was a Halloween tradition during my youth. Any kid caught would be unceremoniously tossed by the frat boys into a pit of red dye and other unmentionable ingredients. The former Deke house is a residence today.

The prospect of being seized by a Deke was so frightening to me that I never got close; I preferred to hang back with the knots of nervous boys gathering in the neighborhood to plan their assaults. But certain friends of mine, the braver sort, did receive their red badges of courage.

I shudder to think of the legal implications of kidnapping children and tossing them into a dye pit these days. Alas, so many fine traditions have gone with the wind . . .

The Easter Duck

Along the Garden District stretch of St. Charles Avenue, within a few blocks of one another, were two venerable old florist shops, Scheinuk and Chopin. One year Mr. Scheinuk filled his large front picture windows with genuine, live "Easter bunnies" - in addition to Easter chicks and ducklings dyed pastel colors as though they had emerged from their Easter eggs bearing the color of their shells. The word spread, and parents from all over piled their kids in station wagons to see this charming holiday pageant.

Realizing he had a hit on his hands, Mr. Scheinuk repeated the event annually. For uptown kids, the trip to Scheinuk became nearly as important as the Easter egg hunt.

Apparently the creatures were available for purchase, because one Easter Day we were allowed to choose a pink duckling to take home with us. I have no idea what my parents had in mind for its future, but we were captivated by it and competed to "take care" of the terrified creature.

A panorama of chicks, bunnies and ducks in the window of Scheinuk the Florist was the highlight of Easter. We actually adopted a duckling one year.

The pink feathers began to give way to snowy white ones and "Wilmer" grew rapidly. When he (she?) showed a taste for our dog Brumby's food we got Wilmer his own bowl, and from then on he happily gobbled dog food at mealtimes right beside Brumby.

When Wilmer began to rival Brumby in size, my parents decided that a duck belonged with its brethren rather than four kids and a mutt. After plenty of tears and wrangling they convinced us that Wilmer, now a white "park" duck of the variety that cruised the Audubon Park lagoon, would be happier there. We solemnly accompanied him in the back of the station wagon to the park, chose a spot in the lagoon where other ducks were paddling along, and watched as my father placed him gently at the water's edge. We climbed back into the station wagon and drove off, heartbroken of course. Wilmer followed enthusiastically, bounding along the lagoon road behind the car on his floppy duck feet. We returned him, this time with snacks to distract him and to "share with his friends" while we made our escape.

Afterwards, for years, my parents would take us to the park to feed the ducks and visit Wilmer. Of course, being young and still myopic, we always "found" Wilmer (he was, of course, the healthiest and friendliest duck) and made sure he got plenty of the white Sunbeam bread we tossed into the water.

McKenzie's

McKenzie's was a chain of New Orleans bakeries that was no rival to stalwarts such as Gambino's in quality, but due to the convenience of its fifty stores was nevertheless a fixture of growing up in New Orleans. McKenzie's supplied countless birthday parties with cakes and formal events with petits fours – but was perhaps best-known for its king cakes, whose taste and texture I still remember clearly. I always preferred McKenzies' rather plain, sugar-sprinkled Mardi Gras king cakes to more gourmet incarnations, and its version of the pink plastic baby hidden inside each cake (a tradition McKenzie's originated) is the one burned into my memory as the "real" kind. I'd venture to guess that anyone who grew up during those times can recall these king cake babies in perfect detail. How desperately, on king cake day at school, we wanted our carefully-chosen slice to contain the baby! Our mothers probably were not nearly so enthusiastic since it meant they'd have to buy the next king cake for us to carry proudly to class.

In raw, home-spun TV and radio commercials, McKenzie's was promoted by the square-jawed Dick Bruce, who chose various delicacies to describe in cloying detail. The TV spots always ended with him taking a large, greedy bite, to my great annoyance.

The ubiquitous McKenzie's bakeries supplied king cakes for Mardi Gras and petits fours beyond number for society parties, in addition to other delicacies.

Our favorite McKenzie's treat was what we called a "fondue," a gross misnomer perpetrated by my father, who purposely taught us the wrong names for various things merely to enjoy the results. A "fondue" was actually a large, flat Danish with

26

stripes of white frosting and fruit paste in the center. The McKenzie's clerks were always perplexed when we asked for a "fondue," and we wondered why we had to point through the glass to make them understand. My father stood behind us, no doubt grinning with glee.

There were plenty of tears when the chain closed in 2000 – probably not as much for the loss of the baked goods, since there are other wonderful bakeries in New Orleans, as for a fixture of the New Orleans scene dropping away into history, as so many have.

The Corner Grocery

Mouledoux's was a corner grocery of the type found on hundreds of corners about the city before the low prices and product variety of supermarkets drew customers away. Caddy corner from the venerable Perlis men's clothing store, it was run by Mr. Mouledoux, of French or Cajun descent judging by the name. He presided over the store from a raised pharmacy section in the back, but sometimes moved to the checkout counter to help ring up customers.

My mother would send one or several of us to Mouledoux's with a list of groceries, which we would present to Mr. Mouledoux. He would pick the items from the old wood shelves for us; apparently that's the way it was done at all grocery stores back then, before the age of Schwegmann's (more on that later). There must have been no more than a couple of hundred items in the entire store, but people's tastes were simpler then I suppose.

Every afternoon after school we were allowed a "nickel treat" from Mouledoux's and we eagerly would walk the three blocks there together. My favorite was a box of Luden's Wild Cherry Cough Drops, which both tasted good and offered the advantage of being allowed in class since according to the box back then they were "Medicated." Pat Callahan's favorite was a long, chewy coconut bar called a Long Boy Kraut, which tasted awful but lasted a long time. Often, in the front yard of a forlorn shotgun house near Mouledoux's, we would see a small girl with curly blonde hair who reminded us of the little girl in Coppertone billboards with her bathing suit being tugged on by a dog, exposing her tan line. We named her Sally, and for some reason we found talking about her riotously funny. Next door to her lived "the lady with one fat foot and one skinny foot." We always hoped to catch a glimpse of her as well.

Not too many years ago I happened into Mouledoux's, which had survived long after most corner stores had disappeared, reincarnated as po-boy shops or even homes with unique proportions. I told a young man at the front counter about my fond memories of the store, and Mr. Mouledoux. He revealed that Mr. Mouledoux was in fact his grandfather, and that he filled in at the store for the old man sometimes when he wasn't too busy. But he was busy a lot, since he was headed for medical school. He told me that his grandfather had worked his whole life, not taking a day of vacation in something like fifty years, for the day when he might see his grandson attend fine schools, then college, to become whatever he wanted to be. In fact, he had attended the same private schools I had. His father, who served as butcher, had worked just as hard.

My heart sank when he told me the store had been sold and was in its final days of operation. But of course I knew it couldn't last, any more than Mozer's Drug Store further up Webster Street could hold off the onslaught of the big chains. The next time I visited New Orleans, Mouledoux's had become a restaurant and Mozer's, where Charles Buchanan was caught shoplifting candy once upon a time, had been torn down and replaced with a modern house. And so it goes.

Before there were Schwegmann's supermarkets, there were corner stores like this all over the city. The one we patronized was at Magazine and Webster.

Summertime

I doubt there was a better place on earth to summer than along the bays and beaches of the Mississippi Gulf Coast. You didn't have to have a lot of money to enjoy it then, so there was plenty of variety amongst the vacationers. My father, who was straining to put five kids through private schools, was able to rent a house in Pass Christian for a month at a modest cost, and commuted from his office in New Orleans a little over an hour away while we stayed at "the Pass." The community of Pass Christian occupied the eastern shore of Bay St. Louis near the border between Mississippi and Louisiana. The community across the bay is named Bay St. Louis, after the bay itself – so that Bay St. Louis can denote either the town on the west side, or the body of water.

During the summer the water became almost body-temperature – which I loved, being a thin and warm-blooded boy.

Our days in Pass Christian were spent on and around the wooden piers that extended from the shore out into the bay. It

was impossible not to mix with the dozens of families along
the shore, particularly over the course of a month. Many of the
families returned at the same time each year and became
familiar to one another. Some already knew each other from
New Orleans.

In addition to using baited cages, we trapped blue crabs with
shallow nets that sat on the bottom with turkey necks tied to
their centers. Standing on a pier, you had to pull them up
rapidly by their cords hand over hand so that the crabs did not
have time to climb over the edge and escape. They sometimes
did, and of course it was always a "huge one" that got away.
You couldn't see the nets through the murky water, so we were
always excited when pulling them up, not knowing what they
would hold. This went on pretty much all day long, so it
served to fill any slow hours. We also fished for the croaking
fish called croakers, which were delicious to eat, and caught
the occasional flounder, a prized delicacy. The inedible catfish
were always a challenge to get off the hook without being
stuck by the sharp defensive spine, and eels were also a bother,
digging themselves into the mud to fight being pulled up. It
was sometimes hard to distinguish whether your hook was in
the mouth of an eel or caught on a sunken log.

We had a sailboat made of Styrofoam (yes) that a neighbor's
father had gotten by way of a cigarette company promotion –
"Salem" was boldly printed on its sail – and it was nearly
perfect, in that even a modest-sized child could pull it into the
water from the beach and back up on to the sand high enough

to keep it from drifting away after sailing it. Once I decided to sail it all the way across the bay but chickened out just short of halfway. It was probably a bad idea anyway considering the violence of the squalls that swept across the bay on a daily basis. I remember well the squeaking of the mast and centerboard against the Styrofoam and its tendency to rub off patches of skin, one of the boat's few flaws.

Years later, before a neighborhood kid cracked the boat in half by jumping onto it in a swimming pool, I remember it functioning as a ferry during a New Orleans flood. It served us well.

My father typically borrowed a motorboat from his cousin Walker for the month. He taught us to water-ski the first year we were there, and skiing became one of the joys of the summers at the Pass. Every so often we were all recruited to clean the bottom of the boat, which collected sharp, stubborn barnacles on its hull. We had to swim underneath it, holding our breath, to get at the ones near the center.

Every afternoon at nearly the same time, a squall would sweep across the bay. Its leading wall of rain was so distinct that we could race it up the pier and across the lawns back to our rented home, which was a block away from the bay front (we always lost). Even as we aged we were forced to take a nap during the afternoon, mostly so my parents could do the same without worrying about someone getting a fishhook in the eye, and while we always fought sleep we usually succumbed, exhausted.

The kids along the row of bay front homes inevitably found one another and formed an extended pack. The teenagers loitered at night flirting and giggling until their parents called them in.

Back then you could get a nickel for turning in "deposit" bottles, and one summer we found an empty lot littered with bottles that we collected and took to a small country store, exchanging them for loads of candy. We were ecstatic. It's funny how those things left me more excited than, say, a new car does now.

In addition to the Pass, I spent a couple of summers on Mobile Bay with the big, happy Conway family of New Orleans, and the bay-centered life there was even more rich and developed than it was at the Pass.

The most memorable activity was flounder-gigging, done at night by the light of Coleman lanterns when the tide was low. During a certain part of the season the plate-flat fish would swim in to sleep on the muddy sand, their outlines barely visible through the shallow water. If you were careful and quiet enough and had a practiced eye you could spot one and spear it with a pointed gig, then lift it flapping crazily and drop it into your net. There are few memories more beautiful to me than the one of lamp-lit families moving silently across the shallows of the bay.

Summer days on the coastal bays were spent swimming, crabbing and fishing from piers extending out from the shore. Pass Christian, Bay St. Louis and Mobile Bay were favorite summer getaways.

On rare occasions it seemed every creature in Mobile Bay would head for shore to crowd the shallows in teeming masses, and a joyful hysteria would spread through the community as we hauled in crabs, shrimp and flounders by the truckload. This was known as a "jubilee" and was greatly celebrated by both locals and vacationers. Records of jubilees

on Mobile Bay go back to the 1860's. The latest theory holds
that occasionally, a transient phenomenon having to do with
salinity, wind direction and tidal variation results in low
oxygen, driving the creatures to shore – where they flop about
lethargically, waiting to be simply scooped up. GaGa,
matriarch of the Geary and Miller clans, also Mobile Bay
regulars, checked the water on calm nights to divine whether a
jubilee was imminent. When it arrived she would bellow the
news to the entire community along the beach. Once it came
in the middle of the night, and everyone from nine to ninety
was up until dawn collecting the bounty from the sea.

GaGa, matriarch of the city's Geary and Miller clans, entertains a pack of
New Orleans boys on Mobile Bay circa 1967.

Sometimes we headed out into the Gulf with the rising dawn for deep-sea fishing. We generally caught a chest full of mackerel, trout or bluefish. Once we came upon a "minnow-ball," a seething mass of minnows corralled into a ball by feasting mackerel. All we had to do was drop a hook into the water to haul the mackerel up, one after another.

Crabbing was done much the same way as it was at Bay St. Louis, with both cage traps and hand traps. We also caught shrimp, both to use as bait and occasionally to eat, though it was very difficult to accumulate enough for a meal. It was the entertainment of catching them that made it worthwhile, as much as the result. We used a "seine net," with one kid holding a wooden bar at each end. Weights caused the bottom of the net to scrape along the bottom. The net-bearers would walk out from the shore a ways with the net stretched between them; then one of them would execute a wide turn around the pivot person and they'd head back to shore. It was important to keep moving so there was a steady pressure against the net, to prevent the creatures from escaping. Once back to shore we'd pull the net up and spread it on the sand. You never knew what you'd see in the net, so it was a sort of treasure hunt, sometimes turning up exotic fish – such as the little puffers that blew themselves up to frighten off predators, but mostly looked ridiculous.

Some of the older boys developed a method of hand-fishing, tying a short length of line to their wrists with a baited hook at the end. They would scrape barnacles from a pier piling, dispersing a cloud of the tiny animals that lived inside to attract the large striped sheepshead fish that lurked about the piers. Then they would put a snorkel in their mouths, submerge themselves in the murky water and wait – very still, and very patiently. I remember clearly the sight of a lanky teenager bursting from beneath the water with a big sheepshead dangling from his wrist.

Occasionally a ship traversed the bay, creating a wave that made it all the way to the shores on either side. A wave was a rare thing in the bay – so rare, in fact, that when one was spotted (or heard), a loud cry passed between all the kids in the rented homes along the shore: "SHIP WAVE!" The kids would careen out of the houses, even mid-meal and clothed, to dive into the water before the wave arrived. We'd body-surf the wave as best we could, and that was it. But to us, it was more exciting than a fire alarm.

There was a local boy named Danny with a fast, flashy boat, fast enough to allow the more skilled teenagers to ski barefoot – the soles of their feet acting as skis. There was also a lithe, pretty, suntanned local girl, Julia I believe, who became the romantic interest of at least a couple of the New Orleans boys there for the summer. We verified at least one of these romances by sneaking out beneath a pier at night to watch them kiss.

There was constant activity along the piers, with packs of kids who swam, sailed, fished and skied the days away. Sometimes we gathered in knots to walk the red-dirt, gnat-clouded road to a nearby store for candy. We were always barefoot, so it was no surprise when one of the boys kicked a barbed gig and had to have it extracted through the other side of his foot. Catfish spines were the more common threat.

One day, Peter Conway and I were riding our bikes along the main highway, returning from the nearby town of Fairhope, when I decided to cross to the other side of the road. I was hit by a car moving at highway speed and hurled a long distance before landing, badly scraped but mostly unhurt, in the weeds. The bike was obliterated, and the car went off the road and wrapped its front end around a tree. I tried my best to comfort the hysterical driver and assure her I was alive, miracle though it was. It turned out she lived two blocks away from me in New Orleans, and I later tutored her son in English. Small world indeed!

The Conway family moved on to greener pastures, and I remember Peter telling me about their boat in Martha's Vineyard, its motor having quit, being towed to shore by Carly Simon and James Taylor, who were married at the time. Well, you can take your choice, but I'll take that humble stretch of Gulf coastline any day.

Streaking

Also with Peter Conway, I experienced for the first time what live, full-grown, naked girls look like at close range. It's easy to think that American mores are in steady decline, but compared to today those were crazy times. Can you imagine any college campus today where professors sip cups of beer on the green while their students run laughing amongst them in the buff? And this in uptown New Orleans, quite conservative despite the city's general reputation for debauchery.

Peter and I had heard about streaking, and although I don't remember how, we knew it was going to happen at a particular time on the Tulane campus. Sure enough a crowd had gathered by the time we arrived. We were conspicuously the only kids around and we tried to lay low. Before long we spotted a naked boy and girl sprinting through the spectators laughing hysterically, to wild applause. Soon there were other couples, and individual streakers, and a group in hats and nothing else. At one point a nude conga line formed and snaked its way through the onlookers. I remember distinctly those beer-sipping professors smiling happily at the show - old men looking at naked girls! I was shocked, but excited beyond measure. At one point Peter and I were running ahead of a couple, turning backwards from time to time to inspect the live nude girl, when they entered an alleyway between two buildings and slowed to a walk, completely winded. We walked backwards a few feet in front of them getting a good eyeful of the girl until she yelled angrily at us and we ran off, embarrassed but educated.

The River

How could a river play such a seemingly small a part in someone's experience, yet be so important?

The French founded New Orleans in 1718 specifically *because* of the Mississippi, as a perfect base for controlling the river's mouth. Early activity in the city centered around the loading and unloading of products and people near present-day Jackson Square.

But growing up, my family, like most, had very little to do with the river. You couldn't fish, boat or swim in it. It was a working river, too dirty, big, swift and crowded with commercial traffic for recreation. Its shore was virtually inaccessible, lined with rat-infested wharves and floodwalls. Even in the French Quarter there was very little development along the riverfront that invited a stroll or picnic. Once in awhile we played along the levee near the western bend in the river, but this was more about the novelty of an artificial hill in a flat city than the river itself.

Mostly the river was just *there*, a sort of subconscious presence. Sometimes you would hear machinery or the foghorn of a tugboat, or even a calliope from a tourist paddle-wheeler, and be reminded of it. But this was infrequent. The river's presence was more felt than experienced. All I have to do to confirm my awareness of the river is to think of the city without the river - a flat city on a large plain, for example. It simply wouldn't have been the same city, whether we experienced the river in a direct way or not.

I was happy when beginning in the seventies and continuing into the eighties, the stretch of riverfront running along the French Quarter was developed as a tourist attraction, beginning with Mayor Moon Landrieu's "Moonwalk." They say it now draws seven or eight million tourists every year, and at least they will have a clearer picture of what made the city what it is than we did growing up.

Mardi Gras

I won't tread over already well-trodden ground by writing about Mardi Gras except as it figured in our lives as children of the city. Part of our year revolved around this extended festival, and even the schools adapted themselves to its rhythm. But as children, our experience of Mardi Gras was different from that of tourists, or even our parents. For the tourists it was about carousing, and for most adults it was about parties and social events. But for us, other than the annual party on Octavia Street, it was about the parades.

Once upon a time, some genius bolted a long wooden seat to the top of a ladder, thereby creating a wonderful gift to future generations of New Orleans children. By the time my siblings and I were growing up most families had one. It was the father's job to drag it to the parade route and set it up in a good location well prior to the more popular parades.

Three kids can fit in the seat of the typical parade ladder, secured by a round bar that slides through holes cut into its sides. From this vantage point above the crowd the children can not only see the floats in all their glory, but also wave and call for throws, some of which fall into the seat even if the kids are not much good at catching them.

One day some genius bolted a wooden seat to the top of a ladder and a tradition was born. We watched parades a safe distance above the stomping and shoving at ground level as youths scrambled for Mardi Gras doubloons and beads, back when they were considered to have a value. The beads were made from glass in Czechoslovakia in those days.

When we were big enough we were allowed to leave the seat and roam around the ladder, trying to catch throws in mid-air or scooping them off the ground when they fell. Today's kids wouldn't understand it, but in those days beads and aluminum "doubloons" were thrown more sparingly, and they never lay uncollected on the ground as many do these days. For one thing, in the Sixties, the beads were made of glass in Czechoslovakia and were prettier and more expensive. They were actually worth keeping, as opposed to the cheap plastic ones tossed by the ton today.

Back then even the doubloons had a perceived value if not an intrinsic one. A lone doubloon store on Calhoun Street began publishing a guide to their "values," thereby creating a market for them. I can remember when a 1960 Rex, the oldest of the doubloons, was "worth" $100, which was a lot of money at the time. A rare doubloon, such as a red or miniature green one from the Bacchus parade, was greatly prized. Most had lower values of a quarter or so, and even that only on paper. Nobody paid for common ones unless they were building a set, and it was mostly the store that made the money.

Nevertheless, doubloons became such hot commodities that swarms of sometimes aggressive youths began to follow the floats, stomping hands to get at them. There were rumors that some of them installed razors in their shoes, but this was surely an old wives' tale. At any rate some of the night parades became scary, and mothers worried about kids on the ground being mauled or ladders being toppled. Some families stopped attending the night parades. It was probably a good thing when the doubloon store closed and the market dried up. Today, many doubloons lie on the ground alongside uncollected beads as parades roll by, but the parades are safer.

When our family expanded to seven and we moved to a larger home, it was close enough to St. Charles Avenue for us to hear the parades approaching – sirens first followed by the drums of the first band, our signal to join the crowd streaming urgently down the sidewalks. We usually arrived just as the king's float passed – which we cared little about, since the king didn't throw anything and only the grown-ups cared who he was.

It wasn't until I was older that I truly appreciated the marching bands, but even back then I'm sure they got into my blood, as did the dancing flambeau carriers in the night parades, their torches dripping liquid fire (they were once a necessity, but with lighted floats there are fewer and fewer now). As kids, we were mostly interested in socking away as many doubloons and strings of beads as we could. Even the most interesting floats were less important to us than the items tossed from them. An exception was the Bacchus parade, originally maligned as nouveau riche by the old-line "krewes" but greatly appreciated by their members' more egalitarian children. The King Kong float was a huge hit as were later floats carrying "Mrs. Kong" and "Baby Kong," and it was a tradition to attempt to land a string of beads in their mouths. Alas, perhaps the snobs were right, because parade themes these days are more likely to feature Hollywood characters and Hollywood "royalty" than witty satires of local politics or fantasies drawn from classic literature. I cringe to see media personalities rather than local leaders waving from kings' floats. New Orleans has never depended on Hollywood for its culture, and I consider this a bad omen, along with the constant gossip and fawning over movie stars and film people who are all over town these days.

My father rode in the Momus parade, and one of the most thrilling moments of the year was when his float passed. We always learned in advance which he'd be riding. After spotting us through the slits in his mask yelling at the top of our lungs from our ladder, he would first broadcast a handful of doubloons to get those around us scrambling on the ground, then bombard us with bags full of throws.

Every Friday during Mardi Gras season someone in each classroom brought a king cake to class and everyone got a slice, hoping theirs contained the little pink baby that meant they would get to bring the next one. The ones from McKenzie's, as I noted earlier, were rather plain but were by far my favorite, and I remember the taste and sugary grit of biting into a slice as if it were yesterday.

For adults, Mardi Gras is a time of round-the-clock parties and everything from debutantes and glamorous private balls to raunchy underground debaucheries – and today, public displays of flesh. But as kids we knew nothing about these things, nor did we care.

It says a lot about New Orleans that Mardi Gras, "Fat Tuesday," morphed from a single day of feasting in preparation for Ash Wednesday and a long stretch of Lenten austerity into weeks of partying followed by a day of recuperation. Ash Wednesday is all but forgotten, but the frolicsome preparation for it continues, come hell or high water – even, apparently, if it's to the rooftops.

The French Connection

These days kids in most places learn Spanish, but in the New Orleans of my childhood we learned French. New Orleans was originally a French city, of course, and the French heritage was deepened when the Acadians or "Cajuns," Nova Scotians of French heritage fleeing the harrowing British, arrived in the swamplands to the west of the city in the 18th century.

There was enough sympathy with the French that there was purportedly an attempt on the part of the city fathers to rescue Napoleon Bonaparte from his second island exile and transport him to New Orleans, but either he died first or the plan was a tall tale invented later. At any rate, the waiters at Napoleon House in the French Quarter where the planning session supposedly took place will tell you all about it if you're interested.

We started learning French in second grade, so by the time I went to France for my junior year of college, though I had neglected my homework and drifted off in class for twelve years, I had absorbed enough French through osmosis to pass the "recyclage" test that exempted me from further gruesome language studies while there.

We were taught throughout elementary school by Madame Feraud, a cruel and quick-tempered harridan who threw chalk at us or beat us with a ruler if we gave a wrong answer or failed to pay attention. Most teachers liked me pretty well - I was small and rather meek and winsome - but Madame Feraud disliked me with a passion: a real problem when the teacher follows you from second grade all the way through eighth grade, hurling chalk at you the whole time. In response to a stupid answer, many of them mine, she would utter something that sounded like: "Mayskeelaybet." I figured out many years later that what she had been saying was essentially: "My God, but he is STUPID." Imagine a teacher getting away with that these days!

Once she had us memorize a poem in French, but when I stood up to recite it I froze - not surprising for a shy kid. She was merciless. "Mayskeelaybet," she hissed, and ordered me to sit down, with a grade of "F".

It has been around forty years since that day but I still remember the poem. I am not going to cheat, so there will be mistakes here, and I won't even attempt most of the accent marks, but it was very close to this:

"Meuse, endormeuse a douce a mon enfance
Qui demeure au pres out tu coules tout bas.

Meuse, adieu! J'ai déjà commencé ma partance
En des pays nouveaux, ou tu ne coules pas."

I am submitting this for publication as is, from memory, so if
Madame Feraud is still alive she can read it in shame. Of all
my classmates, I was perhaps the only one who ended up
fluent in French, living in France twice during later years.

I must admit that Madame Feraud won my respect during
two shining moments. One of them was when she told the
class about escaping the Nazis by sailing on a small boat from
the coast of France; I suppose she was Jewish. The second
was when a golden statue of Joan of Arc, a gift from France to
New Orleans, was unveiled in the French Quarter (it's still
there) and I saw a tear of pride roll down her cheek during the
playing of La Marseillaise. I felt for her, but not enough to
make up for the years of abuse.

Many outsiders have the wrong idea about the French
influence in New Orleans, believing there are still legions of
French or Cajuns populating the city. I saw a movie not too
long ago starring a famous actor who spoke with a practiced
Cajun accent and referred to every female as "ma chère,"
something I never heard growing up in the city. These
Hollywood imitations inevitably miss the mark and irritate
New Orleanians. The New Orleans accent is closest to that of
the Bronx, transported by Irish and Italian immigrants and
spread widely to become nearly ubiquitous. Even old uptown
families have a bit of this "Yat" accent mixed in with their

relatively modest Southern drawl ("Yat," from the common greeting "Where y'at?," a contraction of "where are you at?" that means "how are you?").

To be honest, French is useful for few things in New Orleans other than reading menus, and even fewer in the world at large. Spanish is a more practical second language, with Hispanics gaining a greater and greater presence nationally. This is true even in New Orleans, as many of the Central and South American-born laborers who moved in to help clean up and rebuild following Hurricane Katrina remain here, to the betterment of the city. As the cliché accurately has it New Orleans is a gumbo, and to me the Hispanics are a welcome new ingredient. The Spanish actually ruled the city for a short while, but not long enough to have a significant influence.

Despite its lack of practical value, I can't say I regret having learned the French language, as it stood me well in my travels and is now considered something of an oddity and a distinction in the nation at large. New Orleans is proud of its French heritage, however faded it has become, and I am too.

The Lakefront

The Lakeview area along the south edge of Lake Pontchartrain might as well have been another country. The homes were wide and flat, built of brick in the Fifties, and odd to my in-town eyes. Their lawns were too large and they were spaced too far apart. Between them and the lake was a wide belt of grass and the main road running alongside the lake.

The lake itself is so large that you can't see across it, so especially to a youngster it might as well have been an ocean. My parents would let us go a step or two down the steps leading into the water – but not to the slippery, algae-covered lower ones, after one of us inevitably slipped and went into the stinky chemical brew the water was then.

Our first exposure to wild fish was here. We scanned the surface watching for round-headed mullets to leap from the water and splash back down. You could catch a mullet with a fishing pole and a ball of bread, but they were crafty and it took patience and plenty of bread balls. I doubt mullets are edible, but you wouldn't have wanted to eat them anyway – not the way that water smelled.

We sometimes drove to the lakefront for picnics and were always excited by the open expanse, something we weren't accustomed to uptown. We rolled down the levee and played running games.

Occasionally we were treated to a lakefront visit at night to see a fountain that changed colors by alternating spotlights. This was an event, a spectacle to us worth a trip all the way from uptown. I believe it was called the Mardi Gras Fountain.

Later in my life, I would know this stretch of lakefront mostly as a place to park with a girl at night until run off by the police.

Further down was Pontchartrain Beach, which came to mean not the small stretch of artificial beach known by this name, but the city's only amusement park. It was owned by Harry Batt and his brother John, one of whose sons was to become a well-known actor, and the other a New Orleans city councilman (my teenage escapades with Jay included literally running into Lee Circle in a car, but I'll spare you the details of this and other shenanigans.)

The best ride at Pontchartrain Beach was the Wild Maus, which was scary not because of the speed of the cars but because its wooden frame seemed so rickety. The cars moved slowly with a clicking sound, speeding up only during the

short, steep descents. But the scary sections were the slow
ones, when the car would jerk violently around corners and
you had the distinct feeling it was going to tip off the track and
fall to the ground far below. There was a rumor that a car *did*
fly off the track once and killed some occupants, but to us this
made it even better.

I was too afraid to ride the big classic roller coaster, the
Zephyr, for many years. The looping "Ragin' Cajun" later
eclipsed it. I was quite fond of the haunted house and the high-
dive act, but the Wild Maus remained my favorite.

There was a delightfully tacky Polynesian bar and restaurant
called the Bali Ha'i, where later we'd drink Mai Tais and
Fogcutters as friends of the owner's son. A couple of times we
were invited to parties in which the whole park was opened
only for us. We felt very special.

Pontchartrain Beach closed for good in 1982 – a sad loss. It
had been one of the largest and bravest private business
endeavors in a city not known for them, and such a wonderful
part of growing up that I commissioned a Pontchartrain
Beach painting with reproductions to be sold through my art
gallery in its honor (see facing page). Jay owns the original.

Until its demise in 1982, the Pontchartrain Beach amusement park was a kid's greatest entertainment destination. A "Pay One Price" (P.O.P.) ticket was pure gold.

56

At the other end of the lakefront to the west was the Southern Yacht Club, the second-oldest in the United States. My family wasn't the boating sort, but many New Orleans kids learned to sail there, and I later sailed with some of them and sometimes was invited to lunch in the clubhouse looking out at the lake. Despite a hint of elitism, not every member was wealthy; many were working hard to put kids through school, so the docks nearby held many modest boats in addition to the fancy ones. The whole works was destroyed in Hurricane Katrina, and the clubhouse burned to the ground; I drove out there not long after the storm to see the boats piled atop one another like toys.

Going "across the lake" for the weekend meant anyplace on the north side, from the community of Mandeville pressed against its shore to a plot of land on the Pearl River. I spent wonderful weekends at many of these retreats, some impressive and others very modest. One neighbor had bought a plot of land outside the small town of Picayune, and we spent some of the best weekends of our young lives there, building forts in the woods, shooting skeet and camping on the stream that ran through it.

The city of New Orleans is mostly about the Mississippi River, but the lake that forms its northern border was experienced more directly. Now, as New Orleanians leave the city for Covington and other communities "across the lake," it figures even more largely.

Maids

In these politically correct times, I hesitate to write about the wonderful women, virtually all of them black, who worked in the homes of many New Orleanians. But to leave them out would be to dishonor them, and so many I knew growing up were worthy of honor. In many cases they were very nearly a part of the family and almost as proud of the children they helped rear as they were of their own.

Cora was a large, boisterous black woman from the toughest housing project in town given to raucous laughter, particularly in response to the antics of my siblings and me. To us Cora was legendary because she had once knocked down and sat on a would-be purse-snatcher until the police arrived. She did as little work as possible and sometimes made the mistake of leaving a telltale pile of cigarette butts in an ashtray in the TV room, where she occasionally snuck off to watch soap operas when nobody was around. My younger brother Chris, being precocious, learned that by threatening to report Cora's loafing he could blackmail her into taking him to the Williams Supermarket on Jackson Avenue and St. Charles for an ice cream sandwich (we had moved from Webster Street by then). It was only a game – she and Chris loved one another – but it always worked. She got her "stories" as she called them, and he got his treat. We loved Cora and she loved us, but Chris was always her favorite, and they kept up with one another long after Cora had moved on to other things and Chris had become a successful young lawyer. My sisters attended Cora's funeral many years later, the only white people there. I am sure none of her friends and family, other than the few my sisters were able to speak to, understood how important she had been to us.

In addition to Cora, over the years we had Lil, whom we also loved, and Beatrice, who spent a stretch of probably fifteen years with us. Bea complained a lot, and looking back I don't blame her, because by the time she got on board there were five kids who left the house a shambles every day. We counted on Bea to wave her magic wand over our trail of destruction, and so did my mother. My brother and I, when we were charged with washing the dishes at night, diagnosed more and more of them as "soakers," meaning they had to soak overnight so that Bea would have to deal with them instead of us. "DissssGUStin!" she would invariably say when she walked into the house.

When she was particularly vexed, Bea would declare that her nerves were "upstirred" and sink with a sigh onto the high metal chair in the kitchen to reflect on her troubles. Many of her troubles, however, originated not with us but with her husband Oscar, a light-skinned Creole who apparently spent most of his time gambling Bea's money away, chasing women and drinking. He was a rogue but a loveable rogue, and as kids we always enjoyed visiting with him when drove up and honked his horn in the early evening to pick up Bea.

Our long-time house maid Beatrice, a fine example of the wonderful, hardworking women who helped New Orleans mothers rear their often large broods of children.

Bea lived right beside the notorious St. Thomas housing project on Adele Street (she pronounced it A-dell). She would often describe for us what were known along her street as "floor shows": public scenes that ranged anywhere from shouting matches between lovers to gunfights between gang members. She took a perverse pleasure in floor shows. To her it was entertainment of the highest order, and free of charge. She didn't worry much about the violence because anyone coming through *her* door would get a 38-caliber slug between the eyes. An ongoing theme was the "sailor-boys" from foreign countries who would disembark from their ships at the wharves eager for jazz and loose women, only to walk directly into the ghetto, where they were promptly robbed and beaten. She'd see them flying down the street in their white uniforms, followed closely by a swarm of thugs.

The labels Bea wrote in marker on the storage bags of leftovers in the freezer were a source of delight. I remember among others the "Swimps" - shrimp, to the unenlightened. She once left a note by the phone saying "the cutlets is ready" - meaning, we learned later, that a mechanic had called to say that our Oldsmobile Cutlass was ready to be picked up. There was the note that said "Mis Lyman I cant cook this fish, it flesh be yella and it smell rank." Bea called mashed potatoes "oshpotatoes," and I never knew what she meant until years later it hit me: "Irish potatoes." The Irish had flooded the city in the 19th century, and had apparently become associated with their staple food.

Bea quit several times in disgust, but always came back. Once our neighbors, who were good friends, attempted to scoop her up, as reliable maids were valued highly. Their attempt was unsuccessful but my mother never forgot it.

The end of Bea's service with us was a sad affair. My parents threw a party every New Year's Eve for around sixty friends that had become a regular event. The run-up to the party was always chaotic, and while the first floor of our home was spotless the upstairs was a wreck. I suppose the party preparations had used up the last of Bea's patience, because during the party that night she took at least one bejeweled guest on a guided tour of the second floor, including my parents' disastrous bathroom. "DisssGUStin!" Bea announced. She simply wanted someone, anyone, to understand what she faced on a day-to-day basis, I'm sure. But the guest apprised my mother of her private tour, and that was it for Bea.

An aside about my parents' New Years party: we children were assigned the job of opening the door for guests and taking their coats upstairs to pile them on my parents' bed. After that we had our own mission, sugar-fueled with "Shirley Temples" mixed by Jupiter, a beloved bartender with two-toned skin from a bad burn earlier in his life. One of us would tape a piece of paper to the back of one of the formally-dressed guests. The others would then compete to be the first to find it. If the guest were particularly ugly or weird you got extra credit.

My grandmother had a faithful retainer named David who for thirty years served as gardener, party bartender, cook, driver and more. She and David were utterly devoted to one another. Back in the day there was a practice called "toting" – a bit difficult to distinguish from theft but nevertheless different in the minds of its practitioners. Toting meant stealing just enough here and there to spice up your compensation but without really hurting your employer too badly. Food, for example, or an occasional silver fork. Once, David was caught outright with his hand in the till and was sternly confronted with his crime. His answer says it all: "Aw Mrs. Manget, *everybody* tote a *little* bit!" She let it pass.

I was with my best friend when he went to visit, post-Katrina, the mud-filled home of the elderly black woman who had worked as a maid in his home for decades. By sheer chance she happened to arrive at this exact moment in the car of her daughter after months away in Houston, to see her wrecked home for the first time. His efforts to comfort her were what you might expect someone to show for a beloved grandmother. I remember the trip he made to New Orleans to baptize his golden-haired first child in *her* church in the tough Ninth Ward, so she could shine with pride amongst her longtime church friends.

I have mentioned the Batt family. Their own housekeeper was a wire-thin force of nature who was far more strict than the charming Mrs. Batt. Oralee wouldn't hesitate to dress down the Batt boys, or even their friends if we were out of line. And she had full authority to do it.

These women worked hard for many, many years, for not very much money. But as they were mostly unschooled and unskilled, in a city where jobs were hard to get, these positions allowed them to feed their families. And what I hope is clear is that at least in my experience there was a bond that went far beyond the usual one between a family and an employee that made the life of each richer.

Ray's Rollerama

I was small, but fast on roller skates, so I won't forget Ray's Rollerama anytime soon. I usually won the big race held at every birthday party, until a chubby but quick boy named Chris Johnson began to share the victories with me (later in life, he would head up the successful project to illuminate the Mississippi River Bridge).

Ray's Rollerama was located on Jefferson Highway out towards Ochsner Hospital, where I was born. I would give my right arm for a film of one of those Ray's Rollerama birthday parties in 1969. The music was pretty much what we were hearing at the time on the AM station WTIX, including "bubble-gum" classics such as "Dizzy" (Tommy Roe), and certain hits you can still hear today, including "Sweet Caroline" (Neil Diamond) and "Crimson and Clover" (Tommy James and the Shondells). The moms had big hair or bobs and dresses to just above the knees. Our own clothes were hideous, if the old photos I've seen are any indication. And yes, there was a disco ball.

Ray's Rollerama birthday parties were generally considered the "best" kind. We clunked around in our boot skates, did the Hokey Pokey and ate Brown's Velvet ice cream from small paper cartons with wooden spoons.

Kids had all sorts of birthday parties but Ray's Rollerama parties were generally considered the best. You'd first trade in your shoes for a pair of boot skates stored in cubbyholes behind a wooden counter. Then you'd have free skating for a while, with the boys frequently being dressed down by floor referees for trying to upend one another, and boys and girls practicing their first awkward attempts at flirtation. Then in the party area there would be a cake and small paper cups of Brown's Velvet ice cream eaten with flat wooden spoons. Next a series of group games including the Hokey Pokey ("you put your left foot in, you take your left foot out"). And finally, the big race, my personal event. I believe this was the last time I was ever dominant in a sport.

Ray's Rollerama followed most of America's roller rinks and drive-ins into oblivion. But I can still remember every feature of it in my mind's eye, and the anticipation I felt entering the front door and hearing those skate wheels clunking on the wooden floor.

The Avenue

I wonder if there is any other good-sized city in America that is still centered around an original artery the way New Orleans is around St. Charles Avenue? It follows the gentle curve of the river from downtown to "the Riverbend" on the west side and plays the focal role the river itself might have played in a more primitive society. The avenue was the basis for our geography; I mentally divided it into distinct sections.

From west to east, a streetcar ride down the avenue began with the ninety-degree turn from Carrollton Avenue, where the theatrical waiters of Camellia Grill still hold court. The first section ran from there to Audubon Park. Then came State Street, with its big church and mansions. The purple Katz & Besthoff drugstores on Napoleon and Louisiana bounded the next two sections. After that was Jackson Avenue, with commercial establishments running between there and the next marker, Lee Circle. Then through downtown to Canal Street, where the avenue ends at the French Quarter and the streetcars turn around to head back the other way.

The streetcars, it's important to note, were not and still aren't mere quaint relics but serious transportation for both kids and adults. You could get an awful lot of places in New Orleans from the central spine of St. Charles Avenue, including my school, and I depended on the streetcar for years. On a pleasant day, with the window pulled clattering up by its brass pinch releases, there is no more pleasing way to travel in the world.

The prize seat was the unoccupied conductor's chair in back, from which you could watch the avenue dropping away behind the streetcar. It was comfortably foam-filled and spun around on its pedestal, enabling you to observe the entire scene around you. There was a brass pedal in the floor that released sand onto the tracks.

If you were in a group you could shift the back of any of the wooden seats to the opposite side of its base, resulting in two seats that faced one another. These semi-private salons were often filled with raucous kids, including plaid-skirted schoolgirls from Sacred Heart and boys from De La Salle.

The streetcars please the senses in every way: the look and feel of the smooth brass fixtures and varnished wooden seats, the hum and click-clack of the wheels along the tracks, the smell of electricity and the general rattle of the antique construction.

The K&B drugstores were fixtures on the avenue. With its distinctive purple color, the K&B logo was as familiar to New Orleanians as Coca Cola. We made almost daily trips there for everything from milk to medicine. I think most people were sad to see the stores sold off to the soulless "Rite Aid" chain in 1997.

The purple logo of the K&B drugstore chain is burned into the memory of every true New Orleanian.

On St. Charles at Octavia Street was Daneel Park, where parents took their children to play on the swings and rudimentary playground equipment while they watched from benches. The equipment is updated now but the scene is pretty much the same. Most uptown New Orleanians have sentimental memories of this little park.

Further down the avenue towards downtown, between Jackson Avenue and Lee Circle, was a row of Victorian cottages that had been converted into small businesses. Following the crash of the cotton market in the 1940's that wiped out my grandfather, my grandmother Mere (French for "mother") opened a shop where she sold antiques, called the Georgian Shop. On one side of her was a Jewish tailor who had been there since the dawn of time. On the other, eventually, was The Pink Flamingo, a flamboyant gay bar with a drink menu too salacious to quote from here and a jukebox full of Bette Midler and Barbra Streisand. When we were older, we took dates there sometimes on a lark. You could order a "Hole In One," which was an ear piercing performed right at the table.

Across the street was a Burger King, uptown's first fast food, and for some reason my siblings and I considered it a treat to be taken there for dinner perhaps a couple of times a month. This might be a reflection on my mother's cooking, which in a city of fabulous food, was, shall we say, not fabulous. But she had important things to do, such as fighting to save much of downtown New Orleans (including Julia Row) from the wrecking ball at a time when architectural treasures were being knocked down with impunity.

During the Christmas season, my father would drive us along the length of the avenue to peer at the trimmed and lighted

Christmas trees in the windows of the mansions. I well remember the one we liked best every year beside Audubon Park, visible through a cut-glass door that refracted the colored lights and shining ornaments in a hundred brilliant facets.

It was on St. Charles Avenue that I first experienced a jogger. It's amazing now to think that there was ever a beginning to this phenomenon, but to see someone running for no apparent reason was bizarre back then. The avenue has always invited bike riders, and a few times I roller-skated the three or four miles between our home on Philip Street and Tulane University, where I was taking piano lessons. (These were the metal skates you tightened onto your tennis shoes with a key that made a loud, grinding noise on the sidewalks – long before the advent of roller-blades.)

Food

As with Mardi Gras and jazz, I have no intention of addressing a subject so well covered as New Orleans cuisine. But I will mention a few unusual foods important to New Orleanian children of the Sixties.

The Roman Candy man sells candy from a hand-painted, enclosed wagon drawn by a mule. Yes, a mule. In any other city, even a very small one, you'd assume it was a cloying Disney World recreation of a time gone by. Only in New Orleans might you guess that it is completely legitimate – and you'd be right. The cart has been pulled around the city by mule since 1915. It's the same cart, and still mule-powered, not because it's quaint but because it's practical. It allows Ron Kotteman, the current owner and grandson of its creator, to make and sell Roman Candy while the mule takes care of the driving. Patsy the Mule is apparently familiar enough with the route to know which way to go when Ron calls "gyup!"

Why "Roman"? Grandfather Kotteman was Italian but worried about calling his product Italian Candy. It seemed too racial, and the Irish in the Irish Channel, among others, might not buy it. Ergo, Roman. Mr. Kotteman was an ambitious man. He had been run over by a streetcar as a child, losing both legs. His life had been saved by a veteran of the Spanish-American War who happened to be standing by and knew how to apply tourniquets. He was pulled to school by goats on a cart hand-made by his father until third grade, when pranksters repeatedly released his goats in the school, causing his expulsion. He had taken to the streets, eventually selling fruits, vegetables, and finally his mother's candy, which became such a hit that in 1915 he built the elegant wagon Patsy is still pulling around town 90 years later.

We were always thrilled to hear the bell of the Roman Candy cart as it rolled down Webster Street, pulled by a dependable mule since 1915.

The candy is Italian taffy, basically corn syrup and sugar, flavored with strawberry, chocolate or vanilla. When I was a child there were more and more candies coming onto the market that eclipsed it in flavor, but there was something special about these strips of taffy wrapped in wax paper. Maybe it was the wagon, whose bell sent kids spilling from their homes with quarters the same way a call of "SHIP WAVE!" did in Mobile Bay. My favorite was the chocolate, and the best thing about Roman Candy was that it lasted a very long time compared to M&Ms or Sweet Tarts. Only Luden's Cough Drops and Now & Laters, and perhaps a Long Boy Kraut, could compete. But they weren't sold from a wagon pulled by a mule.

Is there a finer-tasting fruit anywhere than a ripe loquat? Apparently there are several varieties of "Japanese plum," but the ones that grow in New Orleans bear small, smooth yellow fruit, many of which are in reach of a jumping child and others accessible by climbing through the branches of the tree. They grow mostly in people's yards, so either you have to know them to harvest the plums or raid the tree uninvited and take a chance on being caught – which was always worth it. Once, I remember, some kids and I harvested enough to sell the surplus. We divided them into plastic bags and set up a table on the street but ended up selling very few, and these mostly to our parents and kind neighbors. No matter, we were happy to eat the unsold inventory. If you haven't eaten a Japanese plum, the New Orleans variety, you are missing out. So try one, even if you have to raid someone's tree.

Then there were the snowballs or "sno balls" of summer, shaved ice flavored with syrups of every flavor. The most famous sno ball shack was (and is) Hansen's Sno Bliz on Tchoupitoulas Street, still using the superb ice-shaving contraption its founder invented to make a bit of extra money during the Depression. I don't remember going there much, probably because there were closer ones that were perfectly fine with us. It was exquisitely difficult to choose flavors from among the dozens on display in colorful bottles, and often we chose two or three, each soaking a different section of the ice for a multi-colored effect. Some sno ball vendors such as Hansen's made their own syrups, and many were wonderfully exotic. There was nothing better than a sno ball in the heat of a New Orleans summer, with the humidity hovering around eighty percent. They remain a highlight of summertime.

Philip Street

With the birth of my fourth sibling we moved from Webster Street to a larger house on Philip Street. Yes, this was the Garden District, but the house was no showpiece. It had been owned by an eccentric psychiatrist, and among its amenities was a long, skinny reception hall that would become our kitchen, a mid-floor fireplace in one room and a totem pole in another. My parents, who were workhorses and very handy, spent most of their spare time over the following ten years working on this house.

We had the incredible good fortune to move into yet another neighborhood teeming with kids. Looking back, this may have been the single most significant joy of my childhood, and much later I would look for an abundance of kids on the sidewalks when choosing a neighborhood for my own family.

My best friend in the neighborhood would later become a hedge fund manager in New York, but you wouldn't have predicted it back then. He was a wiry, tow-headed kid, younger than I was by a few years, and that was probably part of his charm, since I was the dominant one in the friendship. In fact, I became a sort of Pied Piper to the mostly younger kids, an ego boost I needed to face my oncoming adolescence as a shy, smallish, baby-faced boy.

From a parapet on my friend's high roof we bombarded tour buses with large, compressed wads of the tiny, sticky flowers that accumulated along its edges. They exploded dramatically against the windshields when we made a direct hit, almost always bringing the buses to a stop, which delighted us. These buses were known to us as "Ourgals," from a TV commercial in which a spokesman invited the viewer to "let one of our gals sweet-talk you into a tour of New Orleans!" The buses had a low thrum that could be heard from quite a distance. Eggs were the weapon of choice on short notice, and a cry of "Ourgals" in the neighborhood meant to grab a few eggs and dive behind some bushes in preparation for a bombardment. We were eventually caught, when irate drivers began to ring doorbells to question embarrassed mothers.

It's unlikely you'd find a ramshackle house in the neighborhood today, but back then there were two, one directly across the street and one adjoining our backyard. The run-down one behind us was "The Old Lady's House," where purportedly a strange, scary old lady lived hermit-like in one of the cluttered rooms. In great fear we would sneak into the back of the house and creep about among the dusty detritus. After she reportedly died, we explored more of the house but were afraid to go too far, not wanting to come across her body

or some other imagined horror. We once lugged home a
bunch of magazines from the 1920's we had found in an
abandoned room in back and my parents used the beautiful
old automobile ads to creatively wallpaper the boys' bathroom.
My brothers and I can still quote the lengthy ad facing the
toilet.

I have written already about the random lots and loose
landscaping that resulted in secret passageways and hideouts,
and our block was full of them. We took full advantage of these
when we played "the Gun Game," in which we divided the
pack of kids into two teams, each charged with eliminating the
other by killing off its members. I can remember as if it were
yesterday every wall I crept along, every alleyway and weedy
garage and passage through the block from one side to
another. One wall had a poisonous curare plant growing
against it according to its owners, who made sure we knew
about it in order to keep us away. A particularly important wall
ran along the property of a supposedly very mean old man in
an immense mansion, so it was risky as well. We were kicked
out of yards and yelled at frequently.

How did we survive "the Rooftop Game"? The goal was to
summit as many rooftops in the neighborhood as we could,
and some of them were high enough off the ground that a fall
would have meant not broken bones but certain death.
Surefooted and confident, we scampered across their dusty
slate tiles like mountain goats. Obviously our mothers never
knew, but began to suspect something when their roofs began

to leak more than usual. A certain amount of leakage was expected from bullet holes. That's right, bullet holes. I collected a medicine bottle full of lead slugs from roof gutters, some of the thousands fired from the St. Thomas housing project every 4th of July and New Year's Eve.

Eventually one of my school classmates moved into a large, creepy house on Jackson Avenue. He was of an entrepreneurial nature, and together we ran a casino, a candy store and a pinball parlor with exactly one pinball machine. We held for-profit fairs and performed magic shows. We tried a raffle once, but strangers inevitably asked us whom it was to benefit and when we answered that we ourselves were the beneficiaries, they politely declined to participate. We issued homemade credit cards to dozens of kids but were looked upon as thieves by their mothers and usually had trouble collecting. One resentful mother who lived across the street from the pinball machine dryly remarked as we passed one day: "Bing bing bing, fun fun fun!" We even borrowed the 8mm camera of my friend's father (there was no video back then) to shoot film clips of neighborhood kids, and charged a fifty-cent entry fee to showings. None had ever seen themselves on film, remarkable to think about in this age of ubiquitous video. We used a hand ice shaver to make sno balls, which we sold at the showings to increase our earnings.

The neighborhood kids held their own parade each year during Mardi Gras, "the Krewe of Philip." It featured a motley procession of carts, decorated red wagons, house pets and

home-made instruments, and the route was exactly two blocks
long. For the parents it was an excuse for a few extra martinis,
which my father called "clears." He was fond of quoting an old
song: "On a clear day, you can see forever."

The neighborhood parents got along well and often shared
cocktails on summer evenings while kids splashed around in
one of the two swimming pools in backyards along our street.
My parents were conservative and leaned towards elevator
music but my best friend's parents weren't, and they were a bit
younger as well, introducing new music to the neighborhood.
Some grown-up along the street eventually made a cassette
tape called "Philip Street Favorites" which included, I
remember well, Carole King's "I Feel The Earth Move Under
My Feet," Carly Simon's "You're So Vain," Leonard Cohen's
"Suzanne" and Don Mclean's "American Pie."

At one point a well-loved ex-quarterback of the New Orleans
Saints moved with his little boys to a big, pretty home around
the corner from us. He would sometimes play football with
neighborhood kids in his yard. We were thrilled just to be
around Archie Manning, and had no idea we were also playing
ball with the father of two future Super Bowl champion
quarterbacks.

There was a run-down old mansion on Jackson Avenue with
rented rooms in back whose backyard was a tangle of thickets
with an empty swimming pool that served as a nursery for
tadpoles each spring. We collected the tiny toads when they

emerged from the water. The yard was bordered on one side by a jungle of bamboo behind an immense pile of bricks that became the Black Widow Club, one of our favorite hideouts. There was what had once been a squash court in back, packed to the walls with hoarded junk, and one evening it caught fire and burned with incredible intensity. It was only a few feet from the guest quarters of a friend's house, and my father, always brave, positioned himself in the alleyway with a garden hose to keep the house wet. He surely saved it from burning, but I spent some terrified moments standing with neighbors wondering if the collapsing squash court would bury him in flames before the fire department arrived.

Just after college, I would come to live in a dusty one-room apartment in this very building and kiss a beautiful Scottish girl by the pool – still empty and forgotten.

Sports

Readers of a certain age who grew up in New Orleans don't need to be told what it was like to be a Saints fan back in the bad old days, so I won't bother to dredge up those bleak memories.

I didn't go to many games, but one of the very few I did attend turned out to be memorable. It was in the old Tulane stadium, utterly forlorn by today's standards. The Saints had allowed themselves to be knocked around somewhat less than usual, and they had managed to stay within one point of the Detroit Lions. The trouble was they were on the wrong side of mid-field from the goal line, and had two seconds left to score. So the coach did what any other deranged person would: he sent kicker Tom Dempsey out onto the field to attempt a 63-yard field goal, a good seven yards longer than any successfully kicked before. Dempsey had only half a foot, clad in a flat-fronted stump of a shoe. His style was no long, sweeping run to the ball graced by an elegant soccer-style kick, but a few clunking steps and a straight-ahead thwack. He

looked like one of those antique mechanical dolls you put a
penny in.

As we were preparing to head to our cars, collectively shaking
our heads, the football lofted into the air – and just kept going
up. The crowd froze. A murmur rose rapidly into a wild
scream. It was *impossible.* It was . . . GOOD!

*Despite the hapless Saints of yesteryear, many sports fans have fond
memories of Tulane Stadium. I was watching when Tom Dempsey kicked his
record-breaking 63-yard field goal.*

How many other sports records ever stood for over forty
years? I was there, a wide-eyed ten-year-old. Later in life in

another city during one of only two professional baseball games I ever attended, Nolan Ryan pitched his seventh and final no-hitter, a record that may well last forever. So I've been lucky as a spectator.

As a participant I was less fortunate. In junior high I was a small and timid second-string guard on the basketball team. I remember well our crushing defeat by a powerhouse Isidore Newman team led by a skinny kid named Sean Tuohy, who would go on to be recruited by both the New Jersey Nets (basketball) and Cincinnati Reds (baseball). We played on a wavy outdoor asphalt court with chain nets; sports wasn't a priority at Trinity School then, and it showed.

But this didn't mean sports were not a big part of my life and the lives of the neighborhood kids. In some ways the seasons revolved around them – baseball, football and basketball, each in their proper season, played wherever we could find to play them. We played baseball on the empty field of Trinity School when the kids were gone, jumping the spiked iron fence, and football either at Trinity or in the side yard of the Lane's big pink house on Philip and Chestnut.

In later years we'd play basketball in Trinity's gym, which we accessed by following a circuitous route across the rooftop, climbing through a bathroom window, through a hallway and down a stairwell to the door, opening it with a Yale key that one of us had discovered happened to fit.

Probably the best days of my life thus far were spent playing football on the Trinity field until dark with winter coming on, the grass cool on our bare feet. School sports were pressure-filled and intimidating, a foreboding of adolescence and adulthood, but this was sandlot sports for the sheer joy of it, and I would give a lot to experience that kind of intoxicating happiness now.

I suppose fishing and duck-hunting belong in the category of sports, but with my godfather Frank "Smitty" Schmidt they were less sports than tests of both mental and physical endurance. We rarely saw either fish or foul, at least not any that were edible, a record hard to achieve in the so-called Sportsman's Paradise. Smitty was blithely indifferent to the soaking rains, swarms of mosquitoes, frozen limbs and other miseries he arranged for us, but I wasn't. Still, I loved him, so I never said no to a chance to spend time with him in the swamps and bayous, or lost in a storm out in the Gulf.

Shopping

About once every three weeks, my mother braced herself like a pioneer facing west for her journey to the hinterlands: "the Vetrans," as she called Veterans Boulevard, and Schwegmann's supermarket. In a city where most things were within a couple of miles of one another this ten-mile trip was planned with the seriousness of a military operation. "Does anyone need anything? I'm going to the Vetrans!" she would announce. On the Vetrans she would buy the exotic goods unavailable uptown and stock up on groceries at a reduced price.

Most New Orleanians don't know this, but Schwegmann's was more than "our" supermarket chain; it was one of the first anywhere. In the 1950's, the Schwegmann's on Old Gentilly Road was the largest on earth. People actually piled into tour buses for visits to the gargantuan store. This was a time when most groceries were still picked from store shelves by clerks and both self-service and mega-stores were revolutionary concepts. It's hard to imagine New Orleans on the cutting-edge of _anything_, but apparently we were.

My mother would return from Schwegmann's with her station wagon jammed with the store's brown paper bags. Their design is still burned into the memory of anyone who grew up in the city. The empties were used for everything from garbage bags, to Halloween costumes, to masks for embarrassed "Aints" fans. The political firebrand John Schwegmann's personal beliefs and endorsements were printed not only on the bags, but once even on our Thanksgiving turkey. Like many New Orleans mothers, mine had adopted the technique of slow-cooking turkeys in Schwegmann's bags, and this particular bird got a Schwegmann's tattoo.

Though I'm sure he appreciated the savings, my father didn't have much use for Schwegmann's. That was my mother's domain. My father's was Langenstein's, still there on Arabella Street, where he felt a bit more human and the butcher knew how he wanted his steaks sliced. He would run into friends while loading up on specialty items, then pick up his gin at the Prytania Liquor Store, also still extant, right up the street. Wine came from Martin Wine Cellar.

Another of my father's hangouts, often with me in tow, was Harry's Hardware on Magazine Street, where you will still find the men of New Orleans pawing through bins of screws and eyeing power tools. Now it's my turn, walking the block and a half from my art gallery to pick up nails and picture hooks. The big, faceless home improvement stores have not

yet penetrated to the center of the city. But it may not be long:
Walmart has, and is drawing throngs to its in-town location.

*Every week or two, New Orleans mothers would head out to the
Schwegmann's supermarket on Veterans Boulevard to load their station
wagons with value-priced groceries. It was the beginning of the end of the
city's hundreds of corner stores.*

The hardware store at the corner of State and Magazine –
really more of an old-fashioned general store – is still there, and
still stocked with a seemingly random variety of goods and
manned by an ancient staff. This is where my friends and I

bought our pea-shooters, though how they qualify as hardware and how the store has survived is anyone's guess. The Golden Shears barber shop still survives as well, right down the block. One of the barbers has supposedly been cutting hair there for over 50 years.

We bought our Schwinns, including our banana-seat models and later our first ten-speeds, at Herwig's, also on Magazine. Herwig's lasted longer than I ever thought it would and I was sorry to see it finally close its doors.

A man called Mr. Louis cut our hair, and he's still there in the Riverbend area, somehow looking the same age he was in the Sixties. His salon is still called Mr. Louis's Barber Shop, a simplicity I cherish. When we were small he would place a padded board across the arms of the chair for us to sit on. I stopped in there recently, over 40 years after my last visit, and he pulled it out from behind the chair: "Remember this?" I remembered as though it were yesterday.

I have already mentioned Mouledoux's and the other corner grocery stores, and of course there's Perlis Clothing on Magazine, seventy years old and still going, where the terminally-tanned Pat McCausland or Mr. Perlis himself decked out the city's preppies as I was growing up.

Every New Orleanian will have his own favorites, and the ones I've listed are only those that played a part in my childhood. Of course, as an adult, I now have a whole new list of favorite haunts. Some of them, like Domilise's, I didn't discover until my teens, and others don't serve anyone under 21.

It would be easy to mourn the old-time establishments that have been lost, but instead I suppose we should celebrate the remarkable number that have survived through many passing years.

We counted on the Golden Shears on Magazine Street or Mr. Louis in the Riverbend area to trim our youthful locks.

91

Audubon Park

Audubon Park remains the archetypal city park to me and, I suspect, to many native New Orleanians.

The poetically moss-draped oaks are not only old and large, but some seem to have been designed specifically for climbing, with branches that run along the ground before inviting children upwards to heights that make their parents tremble. Several trees we knew as "climbing trees" back in the Sixties are still well known to natives, some of whom take their children to climb the same trees they climbed when they were young.

There was an impressive old steam locomotive built in 1921 that had been placed on display in the park, and my father would take us to climb all over it. As with so many things in New Orleans it fell into disrepair and was vandalized, and eventually it was fenced off, sad and neglected. Later a group of railroad aficionados removed and restored it, and actually drove it back and forth across Louisiana and Mississippi.

The Audubon Zoo was one of those bleak, primitive zoos of the old days, where animals were placed in identical steel-barred cells of concrete, side-by-side. We loved it anyway. Sometimes from our house on Webster Street we could hear what we called the "whoop-whoop" monkeys making their whooping sounds, and once in awhile the roar of a lion.

Even a small hill was and still is an exotic thing to New Orleans kids. Pictured here is Monkey Hill as it appeared in the Sixties.

Towards the back of the park near the zoo was a rather small, deeply rutted mound called Monkey Hill, which was visited by families from all over New Orleans as our local "mountain." We'd roll down it, ride bikes on it and invent games to play on it, and we probably got more joy from Monkey Hill than a jaded Denver resident gets from a 14,000-foot peak.

Also at the back of the park was a pool of playful, barking seals, in a sort of classical arcade. We would sit and watch them cavort for as long as we were allowed.

Both my father and our maid Cora – I don't know which of them originated the practice – would take us on a walk to the park, find a large, sunny patch of grass and scatter a cupful of "candy corns" (these are the waxy, triangular, white-tipped orange candies that have been around since the 1880's, and taste like it). Then, they'd release us to run and collect as many as we could gather. Cora craftily added the rule that the one who gathered the most won the privilege of broadcasting the candy for another search – allowing her to sit for a good hour without doing anything. I can't remember if we actually ate the candies after all of this, but this was before parents (or maids) worried too much about bike helmets, seatbelts, or deadly germs lurking in the dirt awaiting defenseless children.

They also took us to feed the ducks and an occasional swan Sunbeam bread in the winding, scummy lagoon.

There were public bathrooms in the park but we weren't allowed in them. We were never told why.

There was no jogging path in the park then because there was no jogging. Fitness was a later import, and most still don't make too big a deal of it the way people in other cities do. In general, eating and ease are valued above health or appearance, which is why New Orleans frequently makes the top of the list of "fattest cities in America."

Today there's a jogging path with exercise stations, and mercifully for both the animals and their spectators the zoo has been wonderfully renovated. But other than that, Audubon Park is still pretty much the way it was when Charles Buchanan and I explored it barefoot long ago. That's for the best, I think.

Hurricanes

Katrina changed everything, but she came through long after I was grown up and gone, so she doesn't have a place here. I'm going to talk about the hurricanes of my childhood, seen through a child's eyes.

The big ones were Betsy and Camille. Betsy wasn't the biggest storm ever, but she came right up the mouth of the Mississippi and still packed a hard punch by the time she reached New Orleans. I was only five years old, and I have two memories of the storm. The first is looking out of my window in the middle of the night to see, amidst the swirling winds, what looked like flashes of fire. The next memory is venturing outside with my mother early the next morning at the corner of Camp and Webster to see a carpet of debris filling the streets. I most particularly remember the vivid, multi-colored electrical wiring that was everywhere.

Camille was a monster, with sustained winds of 190 mph, but most of her fury was concentrated to the east of us against the little coastal and bay towns where New Orleanians summered.

Not long after the storm my family drove to Pass Christian, where we had spent our summers, for a look at the damage. There was nothing left. What had been a quaint bayfront community was a heap of rubble and brush, with debris-choked swimming pools and front steps leading nowhere. Years later Katrina would flatten this area again, along with a huge stretch of the Gulf coastline.

For all their devastation, however, hurricanes had a good side – at least if you were a kid. They were unimaginably exciting. And because we had parents whom we then believed could protect us from everything and we owned no beachfront property it was mostly a big show to us.

First and most importantly, if the timing was right, school was canceled. This alone was reason for celebration. But an approaching hurricane was far, far better than just another day off.

The grown-ups were busy nailing up plywood and dragging things inside but there was never a sense of fear, at least not that we picked up on. It was essentially a performance on an immense scale, narrated by Nash Roberts, complete with exposition, rising action, climax, falling action and dénouement. Even if the storms veered away from the city we could hope for heavy flooding at the very least. This could mean anything from holding miniature boat races in whitewater gutter torrents to swimming in the streets and piloting small sailboats down them as cars floated by.

In the hours before the storms, as the sky turned an eerie green and low clouds raced across it, the adults had some fun of their own, mixing cocktails and congregating in small knots on the sidewalks and porches between chores of preparation. There was plenty of good cheer. Released from the routines of jobs and homemaking and cocky (until Katrina) in the face of hurricanes, they felt some of the thrill we did in the drama and uncertainty of the moment. Walker Percy spoke of the odd happiness he felt in the face of calamity. I'd like to think that he got at least some of this from his connection to a city that has seen, through the generations, fire, pestilence, occupation, poverty, corruption, racial tension and harrowing crime, yet has miraculously retained its joie de vivre.

Nash Roberts was the wizard of weather for decades, and the go-to guy when hurricanes were threatening the city.

Decay

My visual aesthetic developed at a weirdly young age, and New Orleans was its template. By the age of five or six I found suburban neighborhoods alarmingly ugly and foreign. I preferred old to new, homes packed together to those spread out comfortably, and landscaping that was loose and tropical rather than manicured like a poodle.

I remember visiting the home of some well-off friends of my parents in Lafayette for an extended Easter holiday. They lived in a big brick home on a large expanse of lawn, but it looked somehow wrong to me. A house, if it had to be a mansion, should be tall and blocky, built of wood or stucco and no more than a dozen feet from the neighbors' homes on either side. A patina of age was preferred.

As I grew older it was imperfection I valued most: sidewalks heaved up by the roots of oaks, peeling paint, the green hue of moss on old bricks, weedy mounds in empty lots. New Orleans was an old city and it had shaped my concept of beauty.

By the time I was a teen I had accumulated a collection of old things left by long-dead children of the city: marbles made of china, a porcelain doll's face with accurate glass eyes, parts of mechanical toys from the early part of the century. There was a pervasive sense of continuity with the past that affected me profoundly, if not consciously. I liked old things and old places, decaying places, and Katrina had one effect I appreciated: it slowed, at least for a time, the rise of overly chic boutiques and restaurants. The establishment of the so-called "House of Blues" downtown, a chain "concept" of an old blues club, was a bad sign to someone who had come to love the real thing – the Maple Leaf, or Tipitina's.

I hope New Orleans never becomes a caricature of itself but instead remains simply itself, decay and all, just this side of ruin. If it takes a hurricane now and then to ensure this, then so be it; perhaps not potent enough to wreck lives, but enough to remind us that all is transitory and fading, and therefore beautiful.

A Prayer for New Orleans

"Glory be to God for dappled things," wrote Gerard Manley Hopkins, "All things counter, original, spare, strange." In an increasingly monocultural America, New Orleans, with all its eccentricities, is increasingly important. These days most American kids could move from their home city to another without noticing much of a difference. But not New Orleans kids.

To be from New Orleans, to grow up in the city, remains a distinction. True, there are Hollywood stars on more of the floats, and incongruous, hoity-toity new establishments are beginning to overly impress the locals. The Callahans couldn't afford to rent a house on Webster Street, much less buy one. Mothers don't let their children roam freely till dusk, and many old-time ethnic restaurateurs have nobody to take over their legacies.

And yes, New Orleans kids now carry cell phones. But they also get dragged to Harry's Hardware and Langenstein's by their parents. They eat king cake at school and occasionally are excused to swim in the streets. They play on the only hill in town, climb mossy oaks, and some ride streetcars to school. Their fathers frequently wear tuxedos, and sometimes masks. Perhaps a few still run barefoot through overgrown alleyways and build clubhouses behind abandoned brick piles.

May these things never change. If New Orleans someday disappears into the Gulf of Mexico, which seems more and more likely, I hope people will remember her as a sort of Atlantis, a fabled place that was almost too good to be true. They'd be right.

> *"Times are not good here. The city is crumbling into ashes. It has been buried under a lava flood of taxes and frauds and maladministrations so that it has become only a study for archeologists. Its condition is so bad that when I write about it, as I intend to do soon, nobody will believe I am telling the truth. But it is better to live here in sackcloth and ashes than to own the whole state of Ohio."*
>
> *Lafcadio Hearn*
> *New Orleans, 1877*